highlights

THE BEANEY
HOUSE OF ART
& KNOWLEDGE

SCALA

About the Beaney

THE BEANEY is an Art Museum and Library situated in the heart of the historic city of Canterbury. Following a £14 million restoration project (£7 million of which was provided by the Heritage Lottery Fund) the revitalised Beaney re-opened its doors to the public in September 2012. This fabulous building now provides state-of-the-art exhibition galleries, interactive spaces, explorer areas, excellent educational facilities and a varied programme of events for all ages. The re-opening of the Beaney represents a major contribution towards the development of the cultural offering in East Kent.

Ethos

To enable people to explore, learn, participate and create using the permanent collections, special exhibitions, community engagement programmes and educational activities as inspiration.

Laura Thomas's unique windows of coloured threads in glass, situated in the heart of the building between the main atrium and the café. Commissioned through Museumaker, supported by Arts Council England, the Museums, Libraries and Archives Council, and the Renaissance programme.

Did you know?

- Canterbury Museum had among its early collections 'hairs from the head of Napoleon Bonaparte' and 'the severed hand of Sir John Heydon' from a duel fought in 1600

- Canterbury Corporation bought the museum from Canterbury Philosophical and Literary Institution for £1,600 in 1846

- Donors of objects include the national hero of Peru, General William Miller, Grand Marshal of Ayacucho, who was born in Wingham near Canterbury

- A narwhal tusk at the Beaney was given by Reverend Holman, who took part in the search for Sir John Franklin's doomed Arctic expedition to find the North-West Passage

- A fossil fish given to Francis Crow by the Royal Institute of Paris has an exact matching French half and was probably part of an Italian collection looted by Napoleon

- The Beaney Institute cost £16,000 to build in 1899, when labourers earned about £60 per year, skilled tradesmen £90, surgeons £475 and solicitors £1,340

- An ancient Egyptian staff- head with ibis and cobra decoration was found in digging docks for Nelson's ships at the Battle of the Nile

- Two 17th-century pubs, The Greyhound and The George and Dragon, were demolished to make way for the Beaney

- Excavations revealed ancient Roman 'fast-food' shops on the site of the Beaney extension

- Much of the exterior woodwork was found to have been destroyed by death-watch beetle and had to be re-carved

- The Colpepper Institute in Powell and Pressburger's 1944 film *A Canterbury Tale* is based on the Beaney

- The Beaney displays include over 1,000 objects

History

ON 16 SEPTEMBER 1897 the Mayor of Canterbury, George Collard, laid the Beaney Institute's foundation stone. Canterbury had been left a bequest by former resident, Dr James George Beaney (1828–1891) for the building of 'an Institute for Working Men', with amenities for men from poor backgrounds like his own. Canterbury persuaded the Charity Commissioners to use the money to build a new museum and library premises. The city's museum, founded in 1825, and free library, founded in 1858, had outgrown their premises and a new building was constructed to house their collections. Queen Victoria in June 1899 'kindly consented that the part of the Beaney Institute which would form the Canterbury Museum should be styled "The Canterbury Royal Museum"', and the new building opened on 11 September.

Beaney, the son of a labourer, was born in Canterbury and apprenticed to the surgeon, William James Cooper, brother of the famous cattle-painter. Beaney studied medicine in Edinburgh and Paris before emigrating to Australia. There he became Honorary Surgeon at the Melbourne Hospital, and a pioneer of Australian child health, family planning and treatment of sexually transmitted diseases. A ' bold surgeon' and 'flamboyant self-promoter', Beaney gained notoriety for his surgery and the nickname 'Diamond Jim' due to his fondness for showy jewellery.

Dr James George Beaney

Canterbury Museum had been bought in 1846 by Canterbury Corporation from the Canterbury Philosophical and Literary Institution. Founded in 1769 as the Canterbury Historical Society for the Cultivation of Useful Knowledge, the group had met weekly at the Guildhall Tavern before building new premises in 1825 at Guildhall Street and re-forming under a new name. The 'Phil and Lit' museum had displays of fossils and minerals from Francis Crow, a clockmaker, inventor and geologist of Faversham and Margate; birds, insects, shells and coins; what was described in the museum catalogue as 'Comparative Anatomy'; and objects illustrating 'the Manners and Customs of different Nations'. The Reading Room was available to

Terracotta decoration above stained glass windows on the front of the Beaney Institute. The inscription translates as 'Life is short but art is enduring.'

'working men of the city' for one penny per week. Discussion was taking place nationally about the need for town councils to establish museums and libraries, leading to an Act of Parliament in 1858. That year Canterbury Corporation opened a Free Library.

The Beaney Institute, designed by City Surveyor Mr A. H. Campbell, became a Canterbury landmark and local notables contributed with enthusiasm. Joshua Cox 'furnished all the reading rooms and libraries at his own expense', Alderman Collard gave '200 guineas for the purchase of books for the reference library' and William Oxenden Hammond purchased museum cases. 'Lieutenant-Colonel Copeland, Mr Ingram Godfrey and Mr Pugin Thornton... presented very valuable collections of pre-historic, Roman and Anglo-Saxon antiquities, Italian and English engraving and etchings, medieval carvings in ivory, and other curios'. Dutch stained-glass windows given by Mr Curling to the 'Phil and Lit'

The George and Dragon Inn, demolished to make way for the Beaney Institute in 1897.

were moved to the Beaney. An extension, with a lecture hall and a purpose-built picture gallery, was added in 1934, thanks to a Slater family gift.

Visitors from the 1930s to the1950s recall 'patting the head of a stuffed lion' or seeing the 'hand severed in a duel' that was echoed in the film *A Canterbury Tale* by director Michael Powell. Re-displays in 1961 focused on Canterbury and East Kent material, which was moved to Canterbury Heritage and Roman museums during the 1980s to 1990s. Building improvements have now enabled multicultural and natural history items to return to the Beaney from store.

Before construction began, the Canterbury Archaeological Trust excavated the site, revealing fascinating evidence of past occupation. The Beaney was known to have been constructed over part of the Roman Forum and one of the principal roads. A metalled road surface was found, together with a masonry building thought to be a tavern, a jewellery workshop, the bone-strewn floor and ovens of 'fast-food' stalls and a burnt-down Roman building with a gold bracelet hidden under the floor. Bone artefacts were uncovered from Norman times, and a range of broken bottles and clay pipes from medieval and later inns were found discarded in a cesspit. Also, fine stoneware tankards decorated with names and inn signs. One, dated 1749, carries a relief of dragon-slayer St George and the inscribed name of innkeeper, Henry Saffory: the 'George and Dragon' was demolished to make way for the Beaney.

Mid-eighteenth century drinking tankards, Roman and medieval worked bone items including a hairpin and gaming counters, and a Roman gold bracelet found during excavation of the construction site.

The Collections

THOMAS SIDNEY COOPER

CANTERBURY-BORN Thomas Sidney Cooper (1803–1902) became famous for pictures of cattle, as popular with collectors in the nineteenth century as they remain today. The Beaney collection is of national importance and spans the full range of Cooper's work. *View of Canterbury from Tonford, with Cattle* (below) was painted soon after Cooper established himself as a painter in London and is notable for its exquisite detail of landscape, animals and people. Other works in the collection include *Home Farm* (1844), typical of the paintings most prized by collectors, with sheep and cattle set in the countryside around Canterbury; the huge *Pushing off for Tilbury Fort, on the Thames* (1884), which was painted for Cooper's home at Harbledown, near Canterbury; and *Separated, but not Divorced* (1874), featuring Charlie, a prize Shorthorn bull, three-quarters life size and the largest single animal Cooper ever painted. Small animal studies in oil, kept by Cooper all his life, are a highlight of Canterbury's collection.

Detail of *View of Canterbury from Tonford, with Cattle* by Thomas Sidney Cooper, 1835
Canterbury Corporation commissioned this painting, which was paid for by public subscription and hung in the museum of Canterbury Philosophical and Literary Institution.

***A Border Collie* by Thomas Sidney Cooper, 1838**
Cooper describes sketching a Scottish drover's dog in Cumberland. He kept studies like this all his life and used them in various compositions.

***Donkey, Goat and Kid* by Thomas Sidney Cooper, 1838**
A finely detailed small oil painting on panel, presented through the National Art Collections Fund by Ernest E. Cook in 1955.

CABINET OF CURIOSITIES

THE BEANEY COLLECTIONS date back to the Canterbury Philosophical and Literary Institution, which opened a museum and library at Guildhall Street in 1825. It contained the geological collection of Francis Crow, a clockmaker and inventor of Faversham and Margate, with many fossils and minerals. There were also birds, insects, shells and coins given by Institution members and the public. In 1846 the Institution's museum was bought by Canterbury Corporation. The collections grew and the Beaney Institute was built, through the bequest of Dr James George Beaney, to re-house them.

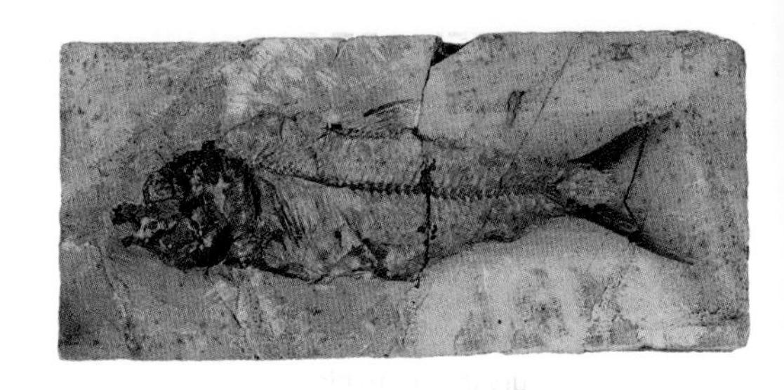

Fossil fish
From the founding collection of Canterbury Philosophical and Literary Institution, acquired from Francis Crow.

Chinese pangolin
An endangered species, pangolins are scaly anteaters that also live in Africa, India and South-East Asia.

Tropical seeds
Collected in British Guyana by Reverend R. Wyllie of Canterbury.

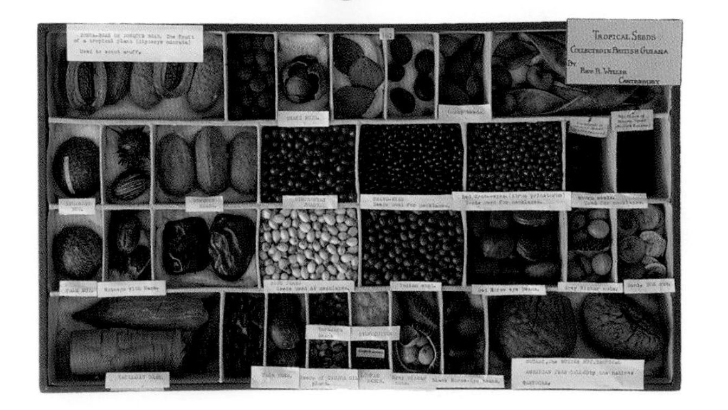

Nautilus shells
These have been polished to reveal mother-of-pearl, and cut to show the mathematical spiral of buoyancy chambers inside. Nautilus shells were much prized by collectors from the Renaissance onwards for their shape and lustre.

ANCIENT GREEK ART FROM VISCOUNT STRANGFORD

PERCY CLINTON SYDNEY SMYTHE, sixth Viscount Strangford (1780–1855), discovered and collected Greek and Roman antiquities. He was ambassador in Constantinople, now Istanbul (1820–24), when Greece was occupied by Turkey. A predecessor in that post was Lord Elgin, who gave Parthenon sculptures to the British Museum. Strangford also gave the latter important antiquities but some came to Canterbury thanks to his son, a local MP.

Portion of a terracotta cornice
Decorated with Grecian honeysuckle and a face, this fragment is from Rhodes.

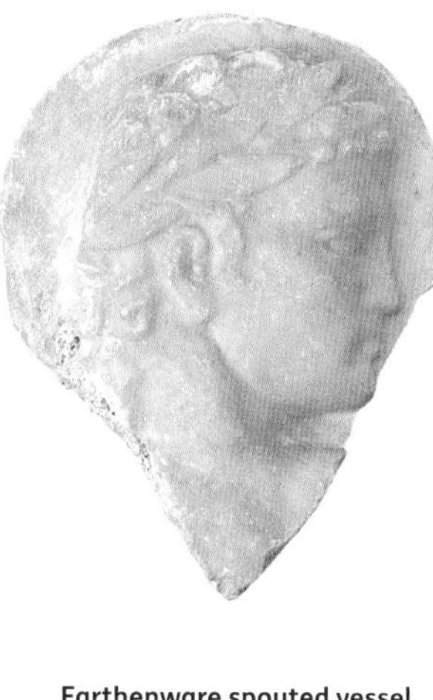

Marble head in relief
Found in 1824 in Rhodes, the Greek island south-west of Turkey.

Earthenware spouted vessel with black glaze
Described as a 'curious black scent jar', this round vessel with handle and spout may be a child's feeding pot. It was found at Athens during a visit by Strangford in 1821.

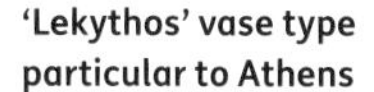

'Lekythos' vase type particular to Athens
Used for funerary offerings, the column represents mythological hero Agamemnon's tomb. His sister, Electra, and son, Orestes, are the two figures honouring the dead. Found in Athens in 1811.

WORLD EXPLORERS AND TRAVELLERS

THE BEANEY'S COLLECTIONS include a range of fascinating items given by people with Canterbury connections who travelled across the world. General William Miller, born in Wingham, near Canterbury, went to South America in 1817 to fight for the independence of Peru, after serving under Wellington in Spain. He became a national hero and was awarded the title of Grand Marshal of Ayacucho. Miller gave the museum a large number of insects and minerals from South America. Items from other collectors include souvenirs of the Battle of Omdurman in Africa and the overthrow of King Theebaw in Burma.

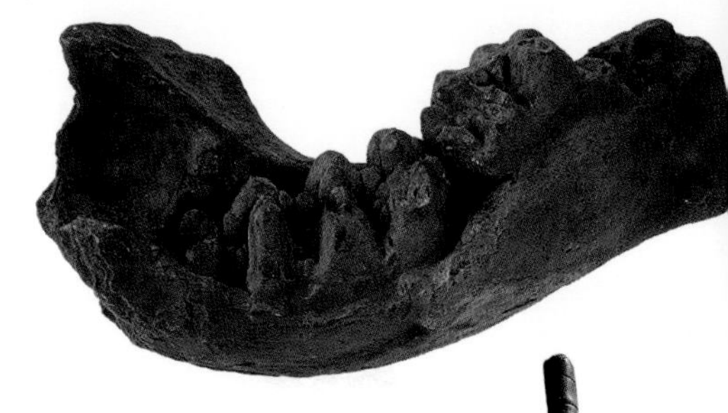

Cast of part of a *Mastodon andium* lower jaw
The original fossilised jaw from South America was given to the museum in 1841 by General Miller and lent to the British Museum in 1845, when it helped establish the new species of elephant ancestor, *Mastodon andium.*

Carved wooden paddle, South Sea Islands
Dates from the early nineteenth century, when the South Seas were beginning to open up to visitors from the west.

Sudanese shield
Given in 1902 by Canterbury resident General Sir James Graham, and brought back in 1898 by his son from the Battle of Omdurman, where the British army massacred Sudanese 'Dervishes', securing control of the Nile.

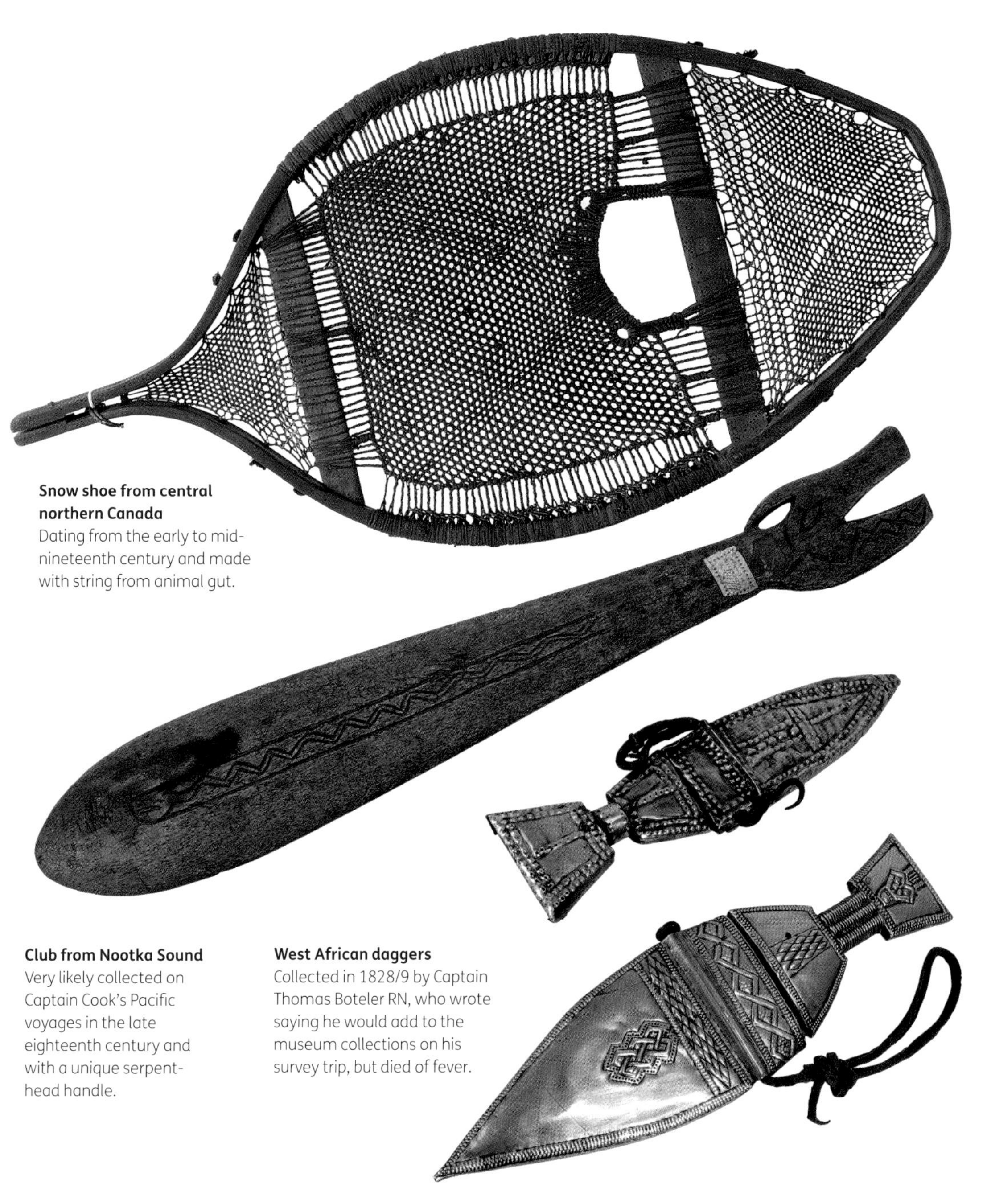

Snow shoe from central northern Canada
Dating from the early to mid-nineteenth century and made with string from animal gut.

Club from Nootka Sound
Very likely collected on Captain Cook's Pacific voyages in the late eighteenth century and with a unique serpent-head handle.

West African daggers
Collected in 1828/9 by Captain Thomas Boteler RN, who wrote saying he would add to the museum collections on his survey trip, but died of fever.

ANCIENT EGYPT

FINDS FROM TOMBS of ancient Egypt, preserved for thousands of years in the dry heat of the desert. European fascination with ancient Egyptian civilisation began with discoveries made during the Napoleonic wars. The Reverend Cooper Willyams (1762–1816) kept some items found by his shipmates, who were part of the Nelson-led fleet that defeated Napoleon's vessels at the Battle of the Nile. Other items given to the museum, mostly small personal objects, were found by the first professional archaeologists to excavate in Egypt. Although there is no human mummy in the collection, there is a mummified cat – a favourite object amongst visitors.

Embroidered Egyptian linen cloth fragment, 400 AD
Given in 1909 by Miss Margaret Alice Murray (1863–1963), who worked with Flinders Petrie and became Assistant Professor of Egyptology at University College London. She was involved in the first mummy unwrapping at Manchester in 1908.

Metal staff head with ibis and cobra decoration
Given by the widow of Reverend Cooper Willyams, chaplain of the *Swiftsure*, and found with other items during digging of docks for Nelson's fleet.

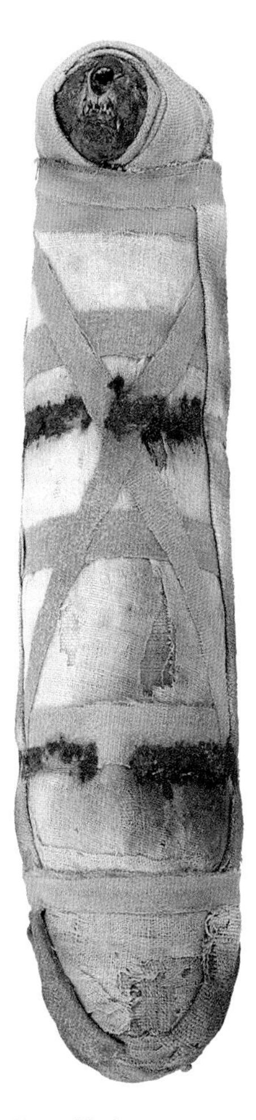

Stone lidded pot of blue anhydrite for storing kohl or galena eye-paint
Found by William Matthew Flinders Petrie (1853–1942) when excavating for the Egypt Exploration Fund in 1899. This dig is famous for being the one where Petrie worked out Sequence Dating to give relative dates to material culture before the introduction of writing.

Lid of a canopic jar
Canopic jars were used to store bodily organs removed in mummification.

Mummified cat
The burial of a mummified animal was an act of piety in ancient Egypt. Cats were associated with several deities and thousands were mummified, only to be exported in the late-nineteenth century for use as fertiliser. Canterbury's example survived and is a favourite with visitors.

ANGLO-SAXON KENT

ANTIQUARIANS, then archaeologists, have been exploring Kent since the eighteenth century. Outstanding among their finds have been Anglo-Saxon items dating from the fifth to the eighth centuries, when Kent was an independent, wealthy kingdom with Continental connections. At first it was a pagan warrior society but in 597 St Augustine was sent by Pope Gregory to bring Christianity to England, and was welcomed in Canterbury by King Ethelbert and his Frankish Queen, Bertha. The Kingdom of Kent was distinguished for outstanding craftsmanship in jewellery, metalwork and glass. Items were also imported from the Continent, whence also came materials, people and ideas.

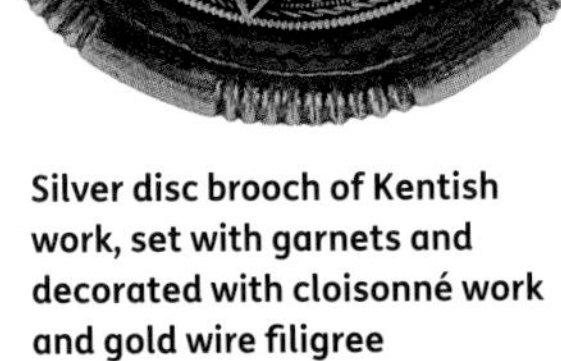

Silver disc brooch of Kentish work, set with garnets and decorated with cloisonné work and gold wire filigree
Found at Kings Field, Faversham, by John Brent (1808–1882), a humanitarian activist, author and antiquarian who was honorary curator of Canterbury Museum.

Cooking pot or bucket with handle
Discovered at Mersham by Edward Hughes in the 1820s and given to Canterbury Philosophical and Literary Society museum.

Square-headed silver-gilt brooch (one of a pair)
Found in 1792 by William Boteler (1745–1818) when 'digging a cellar in the garden of a cottage belonging to me' at Eastry. The 'ancient burying ground' contained many graves with skeletons and 'fibulae, beads, knives, umbones [the centre part or boss] of shields, etc'.

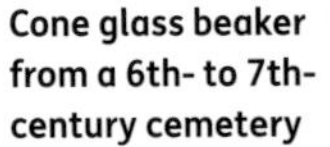

Cone glass beaker from a 6th- to 7th-century cemetery
Found in a gravel pit at Westbere, south of the Sturry-Ramsgate road, in 1931 by Dr A. G. Ince. It was bequeathed to the museum in 1942 by the landowner, Mr Osborn Dan.

THE BUFFS: EAST KENT REGIMENT

ORIGINATING IN TUDOR TIMES, The Buffs (East Kent Regiment) is one of the oldest in the British army, named after the creamy-brown colour of much of its uniform. The regiment's collections used to be housed in Canterbury and are now in the care of the National Army Museum, which has loaned items to the Beaney. On display is a range of items from Napoleonic times to the Boer War, when The Buffs were involved in a succession of battles in defence of British interests and the emerging British Empire.

The Latham Centrepiece of the 3rd (East Kent) Regiment of Foot
Commemoration of Lt Matthew Latham's bravery in saving the King's Colours at the Battle of Albuhera , Spain, in 1811, during the Peninsular War with Napoleon.

REVEREND HENRY LANSDELL'S TRAVELS ACROSS ASIA

DURING THE 1870S and 1880s, Kent-born Henry Lansdell (1841–1919) travelled across Europe and Asia, including Russia, Siberia and China. He wanted to study the needs of local people, as well as distribute bibles and religious tracts. Throughout his travels he acquired various items by gift and purchase. Some were collected for the British Museum; others were presented by his widow to Canterbury Museum in 1922.

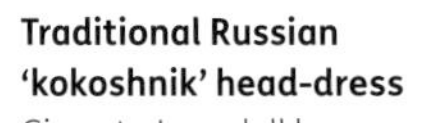

Traditional Russian 'kokoshnik' head-dress
Given to Lansdell by a young Cossak schoolmistress when he 'fell in love with it' and asked to buy it.

Statuette of the Hindu elephant god, Ganesh
Acquired by Lansdell in Jeypore, Chinese Central Asia, in 1889. Ganesh is the lord of success and destroyer of vanity, selfishness and pride. The god's pot belly signifies the bounty of nature

Embroidered trousers
Bought by Lansdell in a Tashkent bazaar 'to be warm and both useful, when tied at the bottoms' for travel on horseback.

SOUTH INDIAN ARMS AND ARMOUR FROM STEPHEN LUSHINGTON

STEPHEN RUMBOLD LUSHINGTON (1776–1868) was a patron and life member of Canterbury Philosophical and Literary Institution. He collected and donated many items to the Institution's museum. Lushington worked in Madras, first for the East India Company then the government, and was later MP for Canterbury. His father-in-law was Major-General George Harris, commander of the Madras army, and it was probably through him that Lushington acquired his high-quality collection of Indian arms and armour.

Head of a steel mace from Mysore, South India, 18th century
A royal symbol of power made perhaps for Khrshnaraja Wodeyar I (1714–1732) and decorated with gold and silver flowers, the shaft housing a concealed knife.

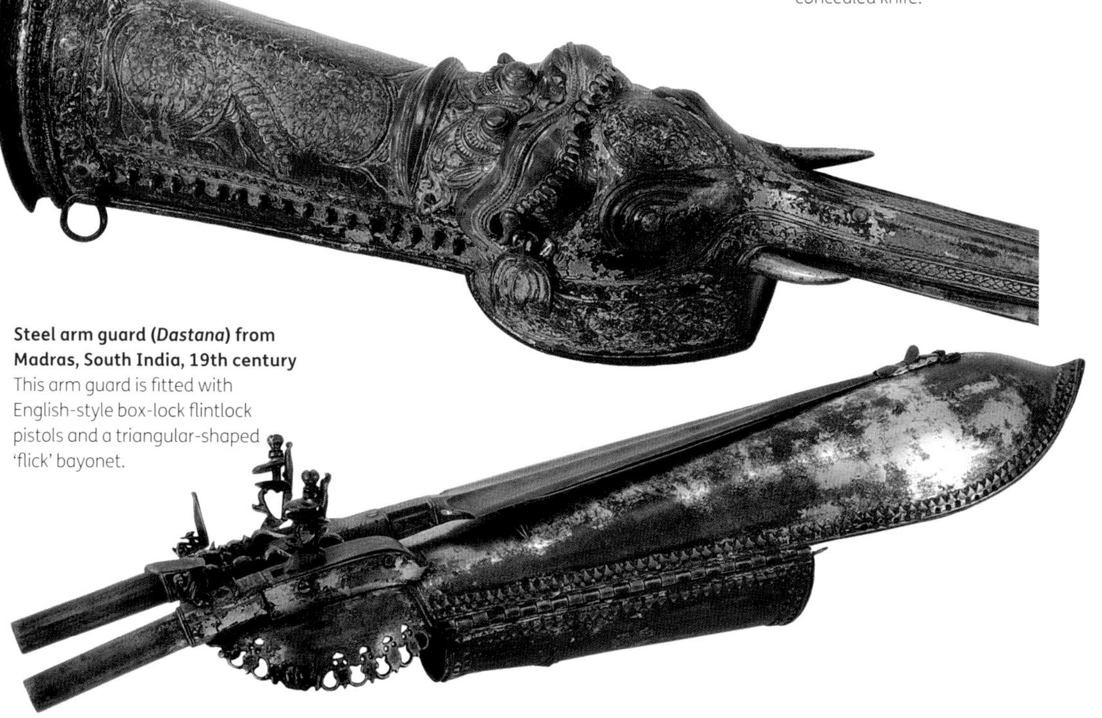

Steel guard of a gauntlet sword (*Pata*) from Thanjor or Mysore, South India, 17th century
The sword guard is shaped in the form of an elephant being devoured by a brass 'makara'.

Steel arm guard (*Dastana*) from Madras, South India, 19th century
This arm guard is fitted with English-style box-lock flintlock pistols and a triangular-shaped 'flick' bayonet.

MATERIALS AND THEIR USES

Obsidian
Naturally occurring glass, formed through cooling of volcanic lava so rapidly that few crystals form.

South Indian shield made of rhino hide
To provide protection at the same time as sufficient transparency to allow one to see the enemy. Acquired by Stephen Rumbold Lushington in Madras during the nineteenth century.

Wooden box
Inlaid with mother-of-pearl from shells, this wooden box shows how natural materials can be put to decorative use. Iridescent shell interiors have been used for combs, fans, boxes and inlay across the world for centuries.

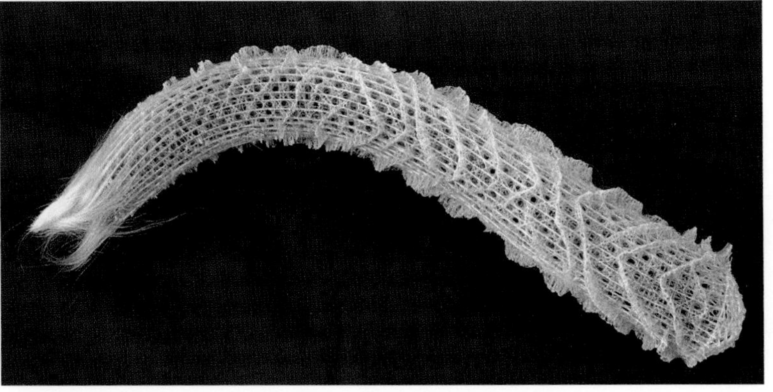

Natural glass
The silica skeleton of an ocean sponge, known as Venus Flower Basket.

DUTCH AND OLD MASTER PAINTINGS

A GROUP OF DUTCH PAINTINGS from the sixteenth to seventeenth centuries, together with copies after Old Masters, was given to the Beaney by Gerard Frederick de Zoete in 1905, with a further bequest in 1932. They were from a much larger collection of European art made by his father, Samuel Hermann de Zoete.

***Virgin and Child* by Bernaert van Orley**
This work was part of a small early sixteenth-century altarpiece, with frame integral to the painting.

Seascape attributed to Hendrik Jacobsz. Dubbels
The ship viewed at anchor from almost dead astern is similar to that in another seascape by Dutch painter Dubbels, leading to re-atrribution of the painting.

Copy by an unknown artist after a *Portrait of a Young Man* by Raphael, believed to be a self-portrait
Raphael's early-sixteenth century portrait was in the Czartoryski Museum collections in Krakow, Poland, until looted by Germans during the Second World War, and has remained untraced.

COLOUR AND CAMOUFLAGE

Exotic blue butterflies
A flavour of the museum's extensive collections of exotic butterflies and moths.

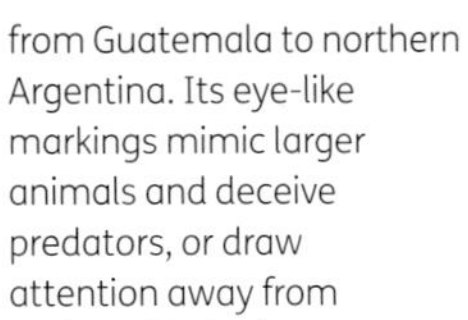

Owl butterfly
Commonly known as the Brazilian Little Owl, this South American butterfly is found from Guatemala to northern Argentina. Its eye-like markings mimic larger animals and deceive predators, or draw attention away from vulnerable body parts.

Azurite and malachite
Hydrated copper carbonate used as pigment by artists.

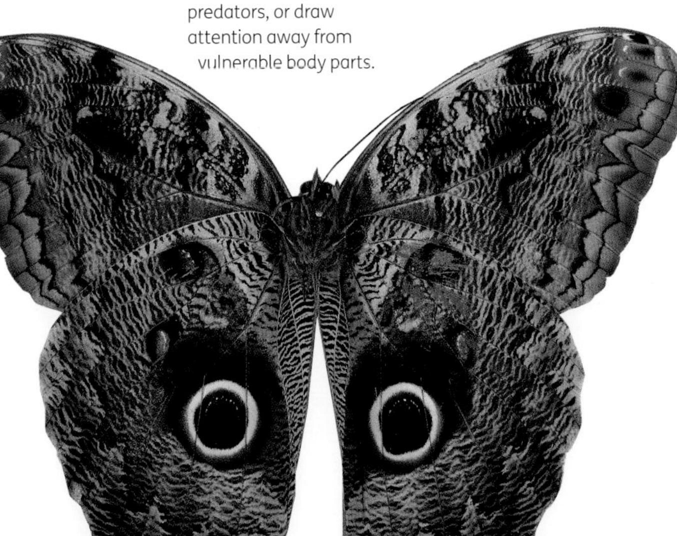

Blue and yellow macaw
A much-loved pet for 40 years, its Herne Bay owner gave this to the museum when it died.

WORKS ON PAPER

CANTERBURY'S COLLECTIONS of fine art are especially strong in prints and drawings. A significant group of Italian prints and drawings, including works by Francesco Guardi and Canaletto, was given to the Beaney in 1899 by Ingram Fuller Godfrey. It had been acquired in Italy during the eighteenth century by his grandfather, John Ingram. Other acquisitions include views of Canterbury and East Kent, such as prints after Turner's watercolours, and work by artists with Canterbury connections, notably Thomas Sidney Cooper and John Ward.

Pencil study of a hop picker by 'Dickie' (Diana) Olivier
One of a group drawn on the spot in 1937 at a hop farm in Paddock Wood, and given by the artist in 1990.

***View of a town on a riverbank*, etching by Giovanni Antonio Canal, known as Canaletto**
One of a large group of Old Master prints and drawings given to the Beaney in 1899 by Ingram Godfrey of Ash.

Drawing of Reculver Church, Kent, in pencil, pen and brown ink by James Ward, 1818
Presented as an outright gift by the National Art Collections Fund (Fulham Fund) in 1986.

PEOPLE AND PLACES

Portrait of Colonel Robert Hammond by Cornelius Johnson, c.1640
Robert Hammond took part in Sir Walter Raleigh's expedition to New Guinea in 1616. During the Civil War he was commissioned to raise a force as part of the Kent Revolt in 1648. He was captured and later killed by Cromwell's forces in Ireland.

***Little Girl at the Door* by Harriet Halhed, c.1910**
Presented to the museum by sixteen of Halhed's former art students in 1930. The artist was born in Australia and came to England as an orphan, aged six, training at the Sidney Cooper School of Art in the city, then in London and Paris, before setting up a studio in Sevenoaks.

***Romeo and Juliet at Reculver* by Walter Sickert, c.1936**
Sickert lived in Kent from 1934 to 1938, staying in Margate then Broadstairs, and lecturing at the Thanet School of Art. Reculver is between Margate and Herne Bay.

***The Canterbury Pilgrims* by Paul Hardy, c.1902–03**
David Paul Frederick Hardy was best known as an illustrator in black and white. His painting of Chaucer's Canterbury Pilgrims is unusual in his work for its large size.

***Canterbury from Kingsmead* by Alfred Dawson, 1881**
An evocative, small example of the many Canterbury Cathedral images in the museum collection.

***Hop-picking Granny Knowles – an Old Hand* by Laura Knight, c.1938**
Hop-picking in Kent and Sussex relied on travellers and people from the East End of London, who arrived each summer to earn some cash in the dirty, laborious task of pulling hops from bines by hand.

DUTCH STAINED GLASS

MR EDWARD SPENCER CURLING of Deal, Consul to the Netherlands under King George IV, collected roundels and fragments of sixteenth- and seventeenth-century stained glass that had been removed from churches and other buildings after the French Revolution. He gave a large group of pieces to the Canterbury Philosophical and Literary Institution, which arranged for a Canterbury glazier to make them into two large windows in 1829 for the new museum in Guildhall Street. When the museum collections were moved to the new Beaney Institute in 1899, the windows were re-leaded and rearranged by the workshop of S. Caldwell and Son, responsible for restoration of the stained glass at Canterbury Cathedral. One of the Beaney windows was removed in the 1930s when the building was extended and remained in store until restoration for current display, along with the well-known staircase window.

The fragments show a range of subjects and styles, from finely detailed monochrome images based on engravings to colourful splashes of angel wings, flowers and birds.

GK
REVERENDISSIMUS AC ILLUSTRISSIMUS DOMINUS
IOANNES FERDINANDUS VAN BEUGHEM
EPISCOPUS ANTVERPIENSIS
Antoen de Roouer met
Anna wielm Aerts
sijn huijsvrouw

HAGHEN

FRANCHOIS DONCK
A° 1615

The journey continues...

IF YOU'VE ENJOYED your time at the Beaney, why not continue your journey with a visit to one of our other museums? Each offers a unique experience with fascinating displays and activities to delight and inspire visitors of all ages.

Canterbury Heritage Museum

Just a few steps from the Beaney is Canterbury's Heritage Museum. Discover Canterbury's history, from millions of years ago to the present, explored through interactive displays in an amazing medieval building. Includes Anglo-Saxon treasures, Oliver Postgate's Thomas Becket storyboard, the Tudors, Joseph Conrad's study, the Blitz gallery, Stephenson's original Invicta railway engine, Rupert Bear and the real Bagpuss.

How to find us

Canterbury Heritage Museum, Stour Street, CT1 2NR
Phone: 01227 475 202
Email: museums@canterbury.gov.uk

Opening times and admission prices

Monday to Sunday 10am to 5pm
Adults £8
Discounts £6
Children free to a maximum of two children per paying adult.
Admission free to Residents Card holders, except for some special events.

Canterbury Roman Museum

Explore the Roman town beneath your feet at Canterbury's Roman Museum. Built around the remains of a Roman town house, this fascinating underground museum offers visitors the chance to stroll through the marketplace, explore recreated Roman rooms and discover amazing finds including a collection of intricate Roman glass flasks and bottles, jewellery and a silver spoon hoard.

How to find us

Canterbury Roman Museum, Butchery Lane, CT1 2JR
Phone: 01227 785 575
Email: museums@canterbury.gov.uk

Opening times and admission prices

Monday to Sunday 10am to 5pm
Adults £6
Discounts £5
Children free to a maximum of two children per paying adult.
Admission free to Residents Card holders, except for some special events.

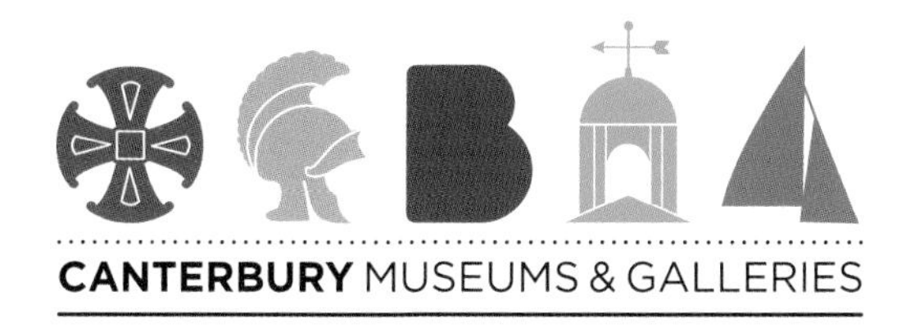

Whitstable Museum & Gallery

Dive into maritime history and explore this enchanting seaside town. Fascinating displays provide visitors and residents with an insight into the town's history, and how it has changed over the years. Discover local stories, the world's first passenger steam railway and memorabilia of Whitstable resident and actor, Peter Cushing.

The museum's art gallery offers a regular programme of exhibitions including touring shows, local history displays and work by local artists. Events include creative workshops and special activities for schools and groups.

How to find us

Whitstable Museum & Gallery, Oxford Street, CT5 1DB
Phone: 01227 276 998
Email: museums@canterbury.gov.uk

Opening times and admission prices

Monday to Sunday 10am to 4pm
Adults £3
Discounts £2
Children free to a maximum of two children per paying adult.
Admission free to Residents Card holders, except for some special events.

Herne Bay Museum & Gallery

Discover the Victorian seaside resort of Herne Bay through local paintings, prints and photos, and exciting finds from the nearby Reculver Roman fort.

Displays include mammoth tusks and fossils from local beaches, coastal wildlife and a Barnes Wallis Bouncing Bomb prototype from World War Two.

The museum's art gallery offers a regular programme of exhibitions including touring shows, local history displays and work by local artists. Events include creative workshops and special activities for schools and groups.

How to find us

Herne Bay Museum & Gallery, William Street, CT6 5EJ
Phone: 01227 367 368
Email: museums@canterbury.gov.uk

Opening times and admission prices

Monday to Sunday 10am to 4pm
Adults £2
Discounts £1
Children free to a maximum of two children per paying adult.
Admission free to Residents Card holders, except for some special events.

For further information about all our museums visit www.canterbury-museums.co.uk

Visitor information

General information
For general enquiries please call 01227 378 100 or visit www.thebeaney.co.uk

Be the first to hear about our events and exhibitions.
Have details of our special events and exhibitions sent straight to your inbox by signing up for our free Beaney e-newsletter. To sign up, visit www.thebeaney.co.uk or speak to a member of staff at the information desk.

Opening hours
For details of our opening hours please call 01227 378 100 or visit www.thebeaney.co.uk

Educational visits
The Beaney offers an exciting programme of events and activities for schools and colleges designed to inspire young people and enrich learning. See the learning section of our website for full details.

Group visits
Planning a group visit? The Beaney offers a variety of talks, tours and interactive sessions for groups. See the groups section of our website for full details.

The Beaney is on Facebook
Remember to 'like' our Beaney Facebook page and keep up to date with the latest news and information. www.facebook.com/thebeaney

Support the Beaney

The Beaney's extensive special exhibitions, lifelong learning and community engagement programmes are only possible due to the generous and ongoing support we receive from a number of individuals, businesses, trusts and foundations. To find out how you can support the Beaney, visit www.thebeaney.co.uk
Your contribution will be much appreciated and make a real difference.

Tourist Information

The Beaney is home to Canterbury's Tourist Information Centre. Our dedicated staff can provide a wealth of information, ensuring your visit to Canterbury is a memorable one. It's also a great place to purchase souvenirs, books and local products.

Our staff can assist with:

- Information about Canterbury and the surrounding areas
- Tickets for top attractions
- Guided tours of the city – including walking and river tours.
- An extensive range of maps, brochures and guides.

For full details, please call 01227 378 100 or email: canterburyinformation@canterbury.gov.uk

The Kitchen

Relax and unwind over a coffee or light snack whilst admiring our fabulous Museumaker window designed by artist Laura Thomas. The Kitchen is located on the ground floor in the heart of the museum. For more information about eating and drinking at the Beaney please call 01227 378 100 or visit our website www.thebeaney.co.uk

First published in 2012 by
Scala Publishers Ltd
Northburgh House
10 Northburgh Street
London EC1V 0AT
www.scalapublishers.com

In association with the Beaney
www.thebeaney.co.uk

ISBN: 978 1 85759 810 0

Editor: Sandra Pisano
Designer: Nigel Soper
Printed in Spain

10 9 8 7 6 5 4 3 2 1